Conversations
with My Mother

"One generation plants the seed;
another gets the shade."

Chinese proverb

Conversations with My Mother

A Keepsake Journal
for Celebrating a Lifetime of Stories

LARK BOOKS
A Division of Sterling Publishing Co., Inc.
New York / London

TEXT:
Ronni Lundy

DESIGN:
Susan McBride

COVER DESIGN:
Cindy LaBreacht

ILLUSTRATIONS:

Retro Clip Art © pp. 18, 20, 22, 23, 35, 36, 38, 39, 41, 42, 43, 44,52, 53, 55

Sears® pp. 10, 11, 14, 17, 19, 24, 28, 31, 43, 45, 50, 51, 54, 55, 56

Library of Congress Cataloging-in-Publication Data

Lundy, Ronni.
Conversations with my mother : a keepsake journal for celebrating a lifetime of stories / [text, Ronni Lundy]. — 1st ed.
    p. cm.
ISBN-13: 978-1-60059-088-7 (hc-plc concealed spiral : alk. paper)
ISBN-10: 1-60059-088-8 (hc-plc concealed spiral : alk. paper)
1. Mothers--Genealogy--Handbooks, manuals, etc. 2. Mothers--Biography--Handbooks, manuals, etc. 3. Oral history--Handbooks, manuals, etc. 4. Interviewing--Handbooks, manuals, etc. I. Title.
CS14.L864 2007
929'.1--dc22

                    2007013066

AARP Books include a wide range of titles on health, personal finance, lifestyle, and other subjects to enrich the lives of 50+ Americans.

For more information, go to www.aarp.org/books

AARP, established in 1958, is a nonprofit, nonpartisan organization with more than 37 million members age 50 and older. The views expressed herein do not necessarily represent the policies of AARP and should not be construed as endorsements.

The AARP name and logo are registered trademarks of AARP, used under license to Sterling Publishing Co., Inc.

10 9 8 7 6 5 4 3

First Edition

Published by Lark Books, A Division of
Sterling Publishing Co., Inc.
387 Park Avenue South, New York, N.Y. 10016

Distributed in Canada by Sterling Publishing,
c/o Canadian Manda Group, 165 Dufferin Street
Toronto, Ontario, Canada M6K 3H6

Distributed in the United Kingdom by GMC Distribution Services,
Castle Place, 166 High Street, Lewes, East Sussex, England BN7 1XU

Distributed in Australia by Capricorn Link (Australia) Pty Ltd.,
P.O. Box 704, Windsor, NSW 2756 Australia

If you have questions or comments about this book, please contact:
Lark Books
67 Broadway
Asheville, NC 28801
(828) 253-0467

Manufactured in China

ISBN 13: 978-1-60059-088-7
ISBN 10: 1-60059-088-8

For information about custom editions, special sales, premium and corporate purchases, please contact Sterling Special Sales Department at 800-805-5489 or specialsales@sterlingpub.com.

Contents

Conversations with My Mother

Introduction

t's a curious thing about your mother. She is likely the person you have been most familiar with all your life. Her voice was the soundtrack of your childhood, her hands the ones that fed you, held you, and dressed you in your first clothes. As a child you saw her daily, and as a grownup your connection to her is apt to remain so instinctive that you don't even think about it. It's natural that you end up believing this is the one other person you really know.

But do you? Probably not entirely. Your life may have begun with your mother, but hers was rich and full of sauce well before you got here. And as you may have glimpsed when you chanced to ask the right question at the right time or when a conversation has taken an unusual turn, the part of her you have seen and valued as her child is really only one facet of a complex and intriguing person.

So how do you get to know this person? You ask her to tell you who she is and has been. *Conversations with My Mother* will be your guide to doing just that.

This book is designed to be a keepsake, a record of dates and information about the milestones of your mother's life, and a repository for some of the photos and mementos that capture its highlights.

But it's much more than a family album. In each section you will find collections of questions designed to open a conversation with your mother about a specific aspect of her life. These questions go beyond the facts of the matter to the sorts of details that can call up lively, specific memories. Many of the questions will encourage your mother not only to say what happened at that point in her life, but also to tell you how she experienced that event, what she felt about it, or what she thinks about it now. It's likely these questions will encourage you to ask others of your own, inspired by the unique story that is your mother's life.

Think of *Conversations with My Mother* as the spark to ignite a rich and ongoing dialogue with a fascinating woman you've been waiting your whole life to truly know.

How to Use This Book

Every mother-child relationship is unique, and so is every conversation. How you and your mother use this book to record the conversations it prompts will be personal as well. Here is some information on making the process and the results meaningful and your own.

How Much to Write

You'll find questions in this book about milestones and people—your mother's wedding day, the names of her grandparents—with blanks for recording these special, straightforward details. Then you'll find questions that will likely prompt responses you can capture entirely right there on the page.

Most often, though, you'll find vivid, open-ended questions, the kind that summon the memories and stories that give your mother's life its texture, weight, and feeling. The richer the vein a question hits, the less likely it is you'll have enough space on the page to record your mother's answer word for word. Nor would you want to. Record what you feel is the essence of the conversation—the evocative details, the special nuggets, the heart of what an experience meant to her. If it's something you want to write more about, turn to one of the "Where it led" pages at the end of the book.

Where it led...

Some answers to questions will need more space, or they may lead to unexpected memories and discussions. The open pages in the back of the book allow you to say more about a certain subject, record a conversation about something unanticipated, or paste in additional photos or mementos. You will notice a place in the bottom corner of each right-hand page in the body of the book where you can indicate if there's more on a certain subject in these back pages.

"Life isn't a matter of milestones, but moments."
—Rose Kennedy

Capturing the Conversations

If you learned that "neatness counts" and you'd like this book to become a formal family keepsake, you may want to keep a pad of paper handy during your conversations with your mother. Jot down notes, particular phrases and words she uses, dates, and other specifics on the pad, then transfer the gist of her answers into the book later. Or you may want to use a tape recorder to get down the whole conversation. Video aficionados may even want to set up a camera and record the process. Just be sure to use a recording method that allows your mother to be completely comfortable and herself while answering, and that frees you to concentrate on the conversation itself, not the transcribing.

If your style is to use the book as more of a journal-like part of the process, making notes and recording immediate impressions directly on the page, writing in the margins and between the lines, feel free to converse and create your keepsake that way.

Picking and Choosing

Not all of the questions in this book will be relevant to your mother's life—and you may skip entire sections altogether—but some of them will definitely resonate. You can choose several or just one. You may find that a question suggests to you a more specific, particular line of inquiry, and so you will create your own question. You may find that in the course of answering, your mother discovers a train of thought she wants to follow. Such serendipitous tangents often lead to the deepest memories or the most interesting revelations. So the first and most important premise when using this book is simply this: Trust your instincts and follow your heart. Use the suggested questions here as a taking-off place for creating your own uniquely personal conversations.

The Art of Conversation

Self-development teacher Robert Anthony has said, "Most of the time we don't communicate, we just take turns talking." This is certainly true in the regular exchanges we have with the people we have known all of our lives. In fact, we often take our mother's turn talking, finishing her sentences or filling in stories we've heard so often we are sure we know exactly how they go. But the first rule of good journalism is "Don't assume!" This is essential advice here as well. Listen with fresh ears to even the

most familiar stories of your mother's life. You may be surprised at what the details reveal. Don't be afraid to ask what seems to be an obvious question. It often turns out that the answer is not what you anticipated at all.

Every Picture Tells a Story

There are places provided for photos from the past, and you are encouraged to dig with your mother through old photo albums or those boxes we all seem to have full of random snapshots.

You will want to avoid getting bogged down in identifying each and every one. That task is better left for another time. Instead, look for photos that seem to evoke a time or era; let your mother's response guide you to the truly important images.

Photos can be potent triggers of memory. You will want to know who is in the picture and when and why it was taken, but also ask for more specific details. If it is black and white, ask what color dress your mother is wearing. Ask how her grandmother's coat felt on her cheek as she leaned on her shoulder. Ask if your father wore aftershave for their prom date. Ask how the house smelled the day of a big family feast. These details are telling in their own right, but they may also help bring richer, forgotten memories to the surface.

In the back of this book, you will find a collection of envelopes suitable for archiving additional photographs or mementos. In one of these you might tuck a dried rose from your mother's first beau, the program from her graduation, a dance card, a recipe, or a newspaper clipping. These envelopes can be kept together at the back of the book, or placed in the pertinent areas with the questions they illustrate. The large envelope can accommodate a CD with digital photos or video as well. You may want to copy older photos to a CD and keep them here. You may also want to take photos of your mother, her family, and her friends at the time of your conversations.

Taking the Time

It may be your or your mother's personal style to take a look at the inviting blank spaces in this book and fill them as quickly and efficiently as possible. Or it might be that you two will want to work your way through the questions here one at a time at different times, savoring each like the individual candies in a Valentine box. You may decide to devote a single day to looking through old photographs with this book by your side to record memories. You may want to involve your siblings in the interview process. You may want to take the book with you on vacation, visiting it over the course of several days. Or you may want to work on it over the span of many months, or a year. Again, this is a matter of deciding what will work best for you and your mother.

The important thing to remember is to create a comfortable space and allow enough time to nurture a genuine conversation whenever you work on the book. Brew some coffee or tea. Sit in comfortable chairs, turn off the phones, and put your daily obligations on hold so you can savor the moment.

This book is not so much about the product you will make, although we hope it becomes a family treasure. It is about the process of truly getting to know the woman you have known all your life.

You Arrive!

DATE OF BIRTH
_____

NAME
_____

CITY & STATE
_____

Were you born at home or in a hospital?
Who delivered you?

Was there anything
unusual about your birth?

Who named you? Were you named after anyone or do your names
have special meaning? Did you have a nickname?

Did your mother sing you a particular lullaby?
Did you have a bedtime story? A special blanket, or a teddy bear?

Do you know when you walked or what was the first word you said?
Are there stories your family told about when you were a baby?

What is your very first memory?

Where it led...

Roots

Where did your ancestors come from and when did they settle here?

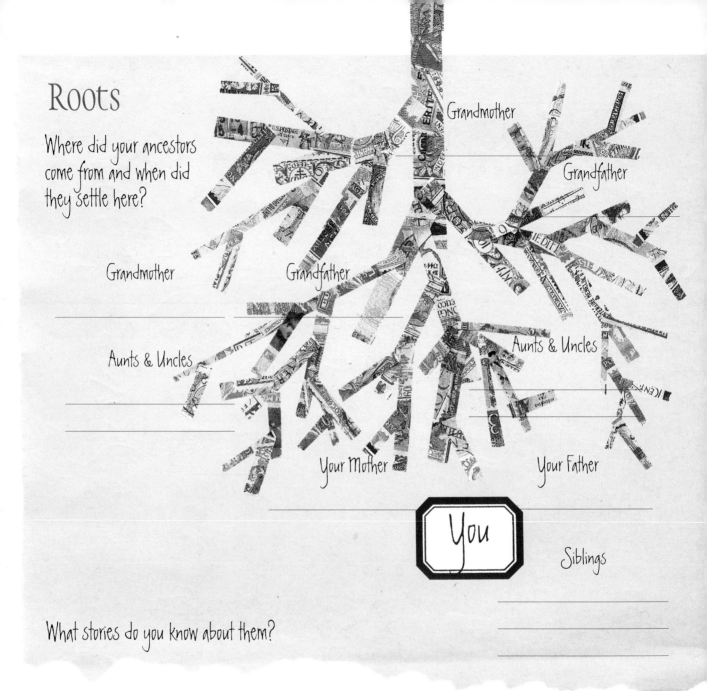

Grandmother

Grandfather

Grandmother _____ Grandfather

Aunts & Uncles

_____

_____

Aunts & Uncles

_____

_____

Your Mother   Your Father

_____

You

Siblings

_____

_____

_____

What stories do you know about them?

Who was the oldest relative you knew?
What do you remember most about him or her?

Who was the most famous or admired
person in your family? Any black sheep?

Did any of the relatives you knew prefer to speak another language?
Did your mother or father identify strongly with their ethnic heritage or religion? Do you?

13

Where it led...

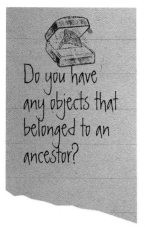

Do you have any objects that belonged to an ancestor?

Did you have a family tradition, celebration, or a recipe that has been handed down for generations?

Is there a trait associated with either your mother or father's clan? Do you think you possess it? Do I?

This page has space for a picture of your great-grandparents or other relatives from long ago. Tell me what you know about any of the people in the pictures.

Grandparents & Parents

If you have photos of your grandparents, use the space provided to attach those images and record information about them.

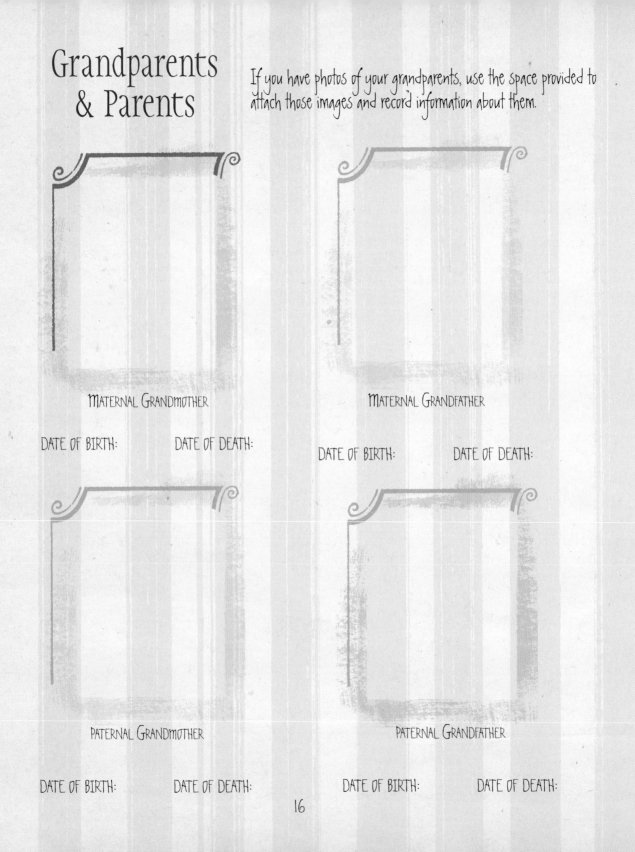

MATERNAL GRANDMOTHER

DATE OF BIRTH: DATE OF DEATH:

MATERNAL GRANDFATHER

DATE OF BIRTH: DATE OF DEATH:

PATERNAL GRANDMOTHER

DATE OF BIRTH: DATE OF DEATH:

PATERNAL GRANDFATHER

DATE OF BIRTH: DATE OF DEATH:

Did you know your grandparents? What were their homes like? How did they make a living?

Did they garden?

Did one of your grandmothers cook anything special for you? Did either of your grandfathers tell you stories or take you on little adventures? Did you have a favorite grandparent? Why?

Did anyone ever tell you that you were "just like" one of your grandparents? How?

What stories do you know about your grandparents? What were their lives like when they were young? What sort of parents were they?

Where it led...

MOTHER

FATHER

DATE OF BIRTH:

DATE OF DEATH:

DATE OF BIRTH:
DATE OF DEATH:

DATE OF MARRIAGE:

Where did your mother grow up? Did she ever tell you about her life when she was a child?

Where did your father grow up?
Do you know any stories about him as a boy?

Where did they meet and when did they get married?
What do you think they liked best about each other?

What did they call one another?

Where it led...

Did your mother like to cook, or sew, or garden? Is there a recipe she made that you would love to taste again?

Did she have any talent, like playing the piano? How did you two spend time together?

How are you like your mother? Different from her? What trait of hers did you admire the most?

Did she have a favorite sister or brother? A best friend?

What did your father do to earn a living?
Did you ever visit him at work? Did he like his job?

Did he like to fish or hunt? Did he make things with his hands or fix
things around the house? What is something you remember him
teaching you?

What quality of character do you think your father most wanted
his children to have? What did you admire in him?

How did your parents enjoy spending their time together?

Where it led...

Siblings

SISTERS

BROTHERS

_____ _____

_____ _____

_____ _____

_____ _____

What was the best thing about growing up in a family the size of yours? What was the worst? Did you ever wish your family had been larger or smaller?

Did you have a favorite brother or sister?
Did you have a cousin or friend who seemed almost like a sibling?
What did you like best about him or her?

Where it led...

Did you share a room with any of your siblings? Did you get or give hand-me-down clothes? How did you feel about that?

What did you do for fun together? What sort of scrapes did you get into together?

Who was the wildest child in the family? Who was the most generous? Tell me about a time that your brother or sister stood up for you. Or you risked something for him or her.

As you got older, who among your siblings do you think changed the most? Did you get closer to a sister or brother you'd not been that close with before?

24

Where it led...

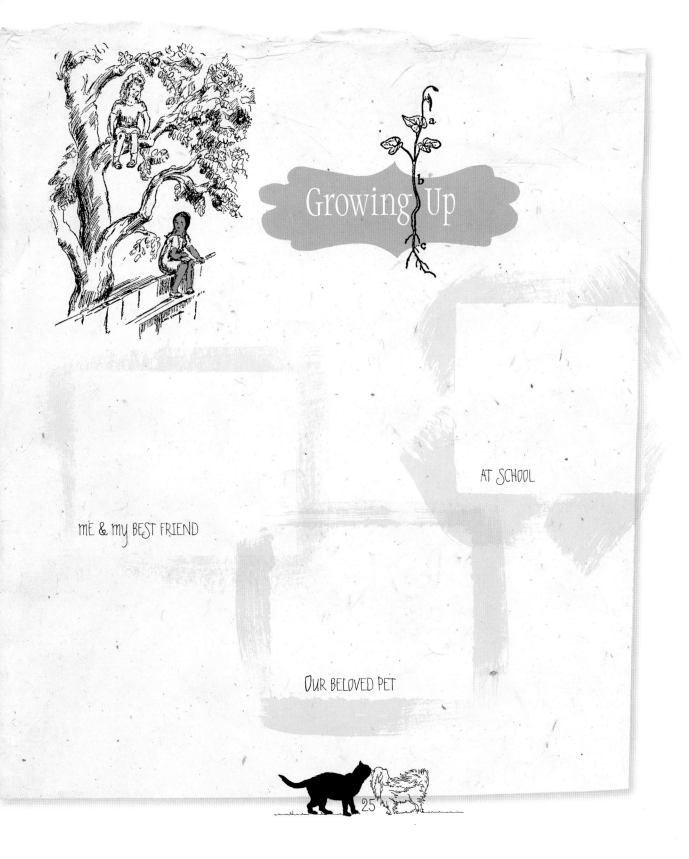

Growing Up

mE & my BEST FRIEND

AT SCHOOL

OuR BELOVED PET

Where did you grow up? Did you live in a house or an apartment? When you stepped inside, did it smell like food cooking, your mother's perfume, or what?

Did you have a room of your own? What did you see when you looked out your favorite window? Did you have a place to hide out when you wanted to be alone?

What did you like best about where you lived in the summer? In the winter? Was there a swimming hole or sledding hill where you gathered with friends?

Did you have a favorite pet? How did you name it?

Who was your best friend? Who were some other good childhood friends? What traits did you look for in a friend?

What did you do for fun together? How do you think your friends would have described you then?

If you could spend an afternoon with one of your childhood friends today, who would it be and why?

Where it led...

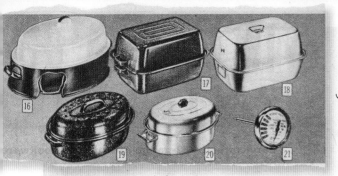

What was your favorite food as a kid? What food did you hate? Did your parents ever make you sit at the table until you had eaten everything on your plate?

What were your chores? What is the first really big responsibility you remember having and how did it make you feel?

What was your biggest thrill as a kid? What was the most trouble you ever got into?

What is your first memory of someone or something important to you dying? How did you feel and how did you deal with it?

Education

How old were you when you started school? What was your school like? What did you do at lunchtime? Recess?

PHOTO FROM SCHOOL DAYS

SCHOOL _____

DATES OF ATTENDANCE

_____

_____

_____

_____

_____

_____

How old were you when you began to read? Who taught you? What was your favorite book or story when you were little?

Did it scare you when you had to speak in front of the class? Did you have spelling bees? Did you win any awards?

Did you ever get sent to the principal or get in trouble? Tell me about that.

What subjects were you good at? Which ones did you hate? What was the hardest subject you ever had to master?

Was there something you were better at than anyone in your class? Did you play sports or were you in any clubs or organizations?

Who was your first teacher in school? What teacher did you fear the most? Who was the most inspirational teacher you ever had? What made her/him special?

Were you a good student?

Where it led...

Did you have many friends in high school?
What did you do for fun? How do you think your classmates would have described you?

Did you have to wear a uniform to school? Did you walk to school or take a bus?
How was school different in your day than in mine?

What did you do as soon as you got out of school every day?
Did you work while you were going to school?

Testing Your Wings

Was there a moment when you felt as if you were truly grown up: Graduation? Your first job? Your first journey alone?

Place a photo here that captures who you were at that time. How did you feel when this picture was made? Proud? Scared? Why did you choose what you are wearing in this photo?

What was your dream for your future at this moment in your life?

Where it led...

It wasn't as common for girls of your generation to even think about going to college. Was this something that you wanted to do? Are you satisfied with how this turned out?

Did you move out of your parents' house? What was the first place of your own like? If you stayed at home, how did life with your parents change?

Do you remember getting your first paycheck? How much was it for? Did you buy something or do something to celebrate?

When did you cast your first vote? Was it exciting? Who did you vote for? Why?

What were your parents' politics? Religious beliefs? As you became a grown-up, how did your beliefs differ from theirs?

Where it led...

When did you learn to drive?
First smoke a cigarette
or take a drink of alcohol?

When you were a young adult, what was your favorite movie, or who
were your favorite stars? What sort of music did you listen to? Did
you go out dancing? How did you have fun?

Was our country at war when you were young?
Did someone important to you go off to fight?
Were you frightened?

Rosie
the
Riveter

Did you or your mother or sisters enlist,
or work for the war effort? How do you think
the war changed your life?

Look again at what you said was your dream for the future. How close do you
think you've come to it? Are you disappointed, or glad about the ways your life
may have turned out differently from that dream?

Where it led...

Love & Marriage

PHOTO OF SWEETHEART

Who was your first crush?
Did he like you? When did you
have your first kiss?

Who took you on your first date and where did you go? Tell me about the best date you ever had. Was there a worst?

Did you go to the prom or another formal dance? Who took you? What did you wear? Describe some other dress-up clothes you wore when going out.

Did you have many boyfriends when you were young? Were you ever "in love" before you met Dad?

Where it led...

Describe what Dad looked like the first time you saw him.
Was it "love at first sight" for you? Him?

Where did you go on your first date with him?
Was it fun? Did you think you'd see each other again?

What did you like best about him then?
What do you think he liked best about you?

Did you ever have a big "break-up"?
How did you patch things up?

WEDDING PICTURES

HONEYMOON

Who proposed, Dad or you? Was your wedding big or small, or did you elope? Why?

Describe what you wore: Did you have something borrowed and something blue? Old? New? Were you wearing perfume?

What was the best moment of your wedding day? Was there a worst or scariest?

Where did you go on your honeymoon?

Describe the first place you lived together as a married couple. Was it fun to set up housekeeping?

Did you have a job? What did Dad do for work? Was it a struggle to pay the bills? What was some way that you had to "make do"?

Were religious observances a big part of your early married life? Did you have different beliefs? How did you resolve that?

Who were your friends when you were a young married couple? What did you like to do for fun?

Where it led...

Becoming a Parent

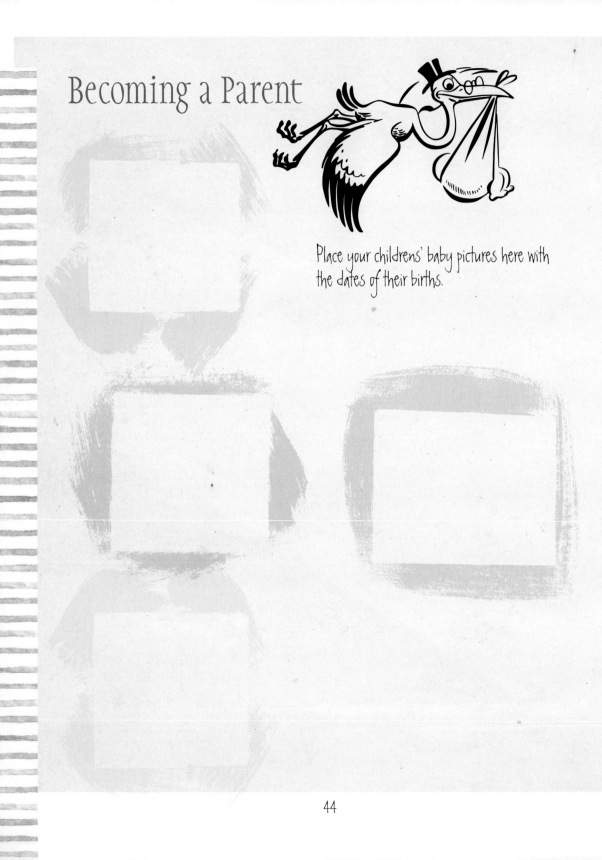

Place your childrens' baby pictures here with the dates of their births.

When you were a girl and imagined having a family, how many children did you want? So how do you feel about the size of our family now?

How did you and Dad react when you discovered you were first pregnant?

In the movies, there's often a dramatic rush to the hospital for the birth of a baby. What was it really like for you?

Tell me about how you named us. How did we get our nicknames?

Where it led...

Having a baby can cause big changes in your life. Did you give up working? Did Dad change his job? Did you decide you would need a bigger place to live?

What were the most difficult and the most frightening things about suddenly being responsible for little beings? What were the most surprising and delightful ones?

What do you think was your best trait as a mother?

How would you describe our family: Close-knit?
Independent? Cantankerous? Funny?
What is our best characteristic as a group?

For each of your children, tell me what you think is his or her greatest strength.
Are any of us more like you? More like Dad? Do you think aliens may have
brought one of us?

What did you think each one of us was sure to be when we grew up?
Who surprised you the most with how they turned out?

If you could change something about the way we grew up,
what would it be?

Where it led...

Family Fun

Photos of family gatherings and holidays

When you were young, what was your favorite holiday? How did you decorate? Did the house smell yummy because of special foods being cooked for it?

When you and Dad married, how different were your ideas about celebrations? How did you resolve that?

Did you enjoy Mother's Day? Tell the truth.

What were your favorite holidays when we were little kids? What about now?

Where it led...

How did you celebrate your birthday when you were a little girl?
How did that influence our family traditions?

If you could, what would you change about the way our family
celebrated? What was your favorite thing about how we did?

Tell me about some of our family celebrations
you vividly remember.

What is the best family vacation that you can remember? What was the most disastrous?

When did we get our first television? What were some of the shows we liked to watch together? What was your favorite program?

What games did we like to play as a family? What were some of the ways we had fun together that you particularly enjoyed?

Where it led...

Moving Right Along

Milestones in the lives of your children

As we're writing down these milestones in your children's lives, tell me how you felt about each of them. Were any of them totally unexpected?

People talk about "empty nest syndrome." How did you feel when your children left home? What did you miss about having us around?

53

With your children grown, did you start a career, go back to school, or do something you'd always wanted to but didn't have the time for before?

How did your relationship with Dad change?
Did you do new activities together?
Was it easier to have conversations?

Some folks move to a smaller house or a different city when they get older, while others feel rooted to the family's home. Tell me why you made the choice you did and what's been best about it.

Tell me about the best trip you've had. Where is the one place
in the world you most want to go?

As you've gotten older, how have your
interests changed? What sorts of
things have become more important to you? Less?

Many women say that once they are past 50 they begin to
feel liberated, freer to be themselves. Is this true for you?
Give me some examples.

Where it led...

A Grand Time

GRANDCHILDREN & THEIR PARENTS   DATES OF BIRTH

_____

_____

_____

_____

_____

_____

_____

_____

_____

_____

_____

Great-grandchildren can go here, too!

While we put in the pictures of your grandchildren, tell me something special or a story about each one of them that we can write down here. Who is the funniest? Who is the most serious? What books do you read to them or stories do you tell? What do you like to do together?

What do your grandkids call you? Where did that name come from? Do you have pet names for any of them?

Do your grandchildren think you are wise? Do they come to you for advice? As they are growing older, how are your relationships changing?

What did you do as a child that you wish your grandchildren could do today? What advantages do they have that you wish you or your children might have had? What problems do they have that are more difficult?

How is being a grandmother better than being
a mother? Are there ways in which it's not as good?

What do you think your children learned from you that made them good
parents? What did they do differently that surprised you?

How do you think parenting in general has changed in your lifetime?
Are these changes good or bad?

What would you like your grandchildren to know about your life
that they perhaps don't?

Where it led...

Collected Wisdom

Photos taken at time of this interview

What accomplishment in your life do you feel is the most significant? What are some other things that you have done that you feel proud about?

Who are the people you most admire? Who are the people who have most influenced you? Why?

What book(s) would you give to your children or grandchildren because it/they had a significant impact on you?

Where it led...

Looking back at your childhood, what strengths of character were instilled in you by growing up the way you did? What fears or problems from then have you had to work hard to overcome?

When you think about your parents now, how do you see them differently than when you were a child, or a younger woman? If you could talk to them, what would you want to say?

Was there anything difficult that happened when you were young that you now see as a "blessing in disguise"?

The lives of women have changed dramatically in your lifetime. Tell me some of the ways you think these changes have been for the better. Are there changes that you think have not been good?

If you could have had the opportunities that your granddaughters have, what would you have chosen to do differently in your life? How do you think that might have changed who you are today?

What advantages do you think you had that your daughters and granddaughters don't?

Where it led...

You have lived through several wars and military actions across the world. How did they affect your life personally?

Do you think the world is a safer place now than it was when you were a child? Do you think there are things that we can do as individuals to influence this?

With growth and shifts in population, the country's landscape has changed dramatically since you were young. How does this look to you when you think about where you grew up—or where you live now?

In your lifetime, you've seen an explosion of technology, from cell phones to space stations. What do you think are the three most important inventions of your lifetime? What new gizmo had the most impact on your life, personally?

Of the famous people of your lifetime—spiritual leaders, politicians, artists, athletes, celebrities—who are the three that you think had the greatest impact on the world at large? How do you think they changed things?

Where it led...

If you could have a conversation
with one important person, living
or dead, who would that be?
What would you want to know?

What do you think are the keys to a good marriage? What traits would you
advise your children or grandchildren to look for in a mate?

What is the best advice you would give for raising good, strong, independent children?

What makes for a good job? Is it salary, enjoying the task, making a contribution to the community, or something else?

Where it led...

What is the key
to having a good life?

What would you like to say to
your children, grandchildren,
and future generations?

Where it led...

Use the following blank pages to continue stories, or to attach photographs or keepsakes.

Where it led...

Continued from page: _____

Subject: _____

Where it led...

Continued from page: _____

Subject: _____

Where it led...

Continued from page: _____

Subject: _____

Where it led...

Continued from page: _____

Subject: _____

Where it led...

Continued from page: _____

Subject: _____

Where it led...

Continued from page: _____

Subject: _____